The Sticks of Inquiry

BJ Ruddy

Harmony Press

ISBN-13: 978-0615945293

ISBN-10: 0615945295

Copyright © 2014
BJ Ruddy

Harmony Press
Charleston, SC

Cover Art: Kate Lallement
http://klallement12.blogspot.com/
http://lallement12.wix.com/artengr

Contact BJ Ruddy at:
www.thesticksofinquiry.wordpress.com

1

To my parents

3

Gatsby's Porch

What dredged lake discovery
upturns opinions drowned
below surface eyes?

We stare on entranced,
the safety of voyeurs with
satchels of sharp stones,

Life viewed, single pane,
opportunity, alive, smash
for shards, blood letting

Beauty down storm drains
rain may blur, couch calls
and kids erase obscenities

The world before chalked on
private property, the surface
lining half empty, half full

The Hooded Fang

This couch is not the
unmapped meridian wild,
London's primordial beast
in cave cell home heredity

It was the lean, hungry
look that Caesar feared
but here among the fat
who could but bleed?

The blood of self trapped
in veins, 18,000 square feet
of shelter from the storm –
how many empty bottles?

Goodnight, goodnight,
let the starlight be bright
as suede seated dreams
are thrown from samsara

*** sleep ***

A jolted bottle bleeds;
up the untamed beast
for suicide suburbia enlightenment,
Chinese takeout and beer

Outside it is, porch, rocker
weather worn and pond bug song;
it is so, so still...listen,
distant interstate love songs

Outside, a Yeats eulogy,
"I have no speech but symbol,"
October wet chill, Achilles,
even, would be silent

No more, just toes and dirt,
the fight for sleep, for work,
for living right angle camera
obscura, the holy truth

So said is sad, hooded
boys shot down images
in the pond's teaching:
om along sister Rosary smile

And like all safe circles
return to suede safety;
tonight I held a homeless
dollar against real breath

Now the poet, the role
rolls hare toes, moist pine
straw disturbed and freedom
somehow slips Irish goodbye

Gone but I'm with cicadas
singing Garcia heart sleeve
love humid October wet
that whets inside appeal

Pave drug dreams, shadows
and simplicity, order known,
all been screamed to no ears
repeat, repeat, reuse, recycle

Wine drunk brother Li Po,
your moon is clouded tonight,
the pond only shadows
so you'll breathe for now

What if the wolves appear,
the company, the fangs,
the pack and my lone neck
here bleeding sex now?

The finished bottle accomplishment,
triumph narratives secure
to propagate the inside dream
against a cold toe's dirt goal

*** moves ***

Inside full body black cat
suede seat Yeats book rests
against blue jean thigh America
holds ancestry in green lights

Green bottles blow stop sign
signals, her bare arms
slide sweet fingers across planes
like a flag that waves on

Rest bottle, on Yeats black
hardcover; know when
like Cummings Buddha now,
Jersey making love to Carolina

The hooded fang exists always
seducing ambiguity with doorknob
marriage vows written, spoken,

stored to know pond silent wisdom

Outside chill, inside sweat,
the wild blurs night mornings in
clean Formica dreams beyond dew
dwelling under panting paws

Everywhere the reason, answers
moon drunk ponds drowning poets
indoor plumbing drains away
the dulling molar's comfort food

The hero's return, death by wife,
for Cassandra's Penelope woven woes
that this sad country slyly
cloaks our night born fang

Find O'Hara energy in time,
find tomorrow's skill in meals of
fried green tomatoes downtown
Holy City bar brawl redemption

What if moves to art poet when
who knew now and fingers until
I remove my shirt bare blue walls,
to kiss with fangs, wordless…

African Violets

What might a man know in the world,
laid to low by an insecure smile,
dew on an African Violet petal?

For all the silence in the universe,
white noise breezes remind her
she's smarter than allowed to be

Or at least I hope they do…
and that's the way of these things:
another routine for lonely mornings

And for What?

Tu Fu asked, at Day's End,
"and for what?"

David Hinton's research
says this question was
asked between 765 and 768 AD,
which would put it between
five and two years
of the poet's death

It's 10:00 at night,
the air is low-country soup,
warm as my beer is cold,
a Sunday's end
and that question burns

The pond is alive with noise
and the line between
fucking and fighting,
when it comes to frogs
and crickets and ducks and
whatever else is singing,
is tough for me to tell

But the point, I guess,
is the living,
something I haven't done
all day

America

They've all gone to look for America – Simon and Garfunkel

When it was our turn
to look for America,
the circumstances were
different but still lyrics turn
like wheels, "Kathy, I'm lost"
and I know I am, what
I used to whisper to you
when you'd sleep till sunrise
at my apartment and
then go home as if to
tell yourself you weren't
sleeping over, not with this
boy who within five years
you'd leave with, counting
the cars on the New Jersey
Turnpike until I-95 five
states away, to look
for America and to
end up lost, or at least
losing, not ten years down
the road, our voices in
car rides of escape that
hang with thwarted ideals,
Paul Simon's bus wheels
rolling under some northeastern
skies that are not this
humid, breathing southern shore,
our coastal dreams landlocked
by interest rates and late fees,
last chances like so many

last cigarettes, we smoked
the last one an hour ago

Food

What's the word for
the way the ocean tastes
on your neck, some
summer indulgence, sun
seared into the memory
of first lips kissed,
first breasts breathing
in young hands unaware
of love but believing
in nature and now
what's the word for
the grace of beauty aged
where depth of presence
means more than
what's spoken at any
present time?

All I know are your eyes
(and yes, your legs
have sure kept up well)
that can cry so hard
at words from me,
that can re-create me
almost hourly,
that can hold me like
the sun holds the pelican
gliding softly over waves
for food

Aloha

A breeze blows 10 p.m.
through wide open autumn,
window eyes, red like leaves
soon to turn, fade, and fall

A man can ask so what of sleep
and reap unconscious answers
forgetting hours never known,
time's fault from the start

Cooler breezes circle, faults break
and heads spin, catching cliffs
to throw broken hearts up over
away into someday's saving sigh

As if this was some distraction:
alarms and chapped lips, hard
for coffee and pens and processes, day
bleeds red over eyes once white

Aloha is the only word left
under a crescent moon, Garcia
out there somewhere singing brightly
let my inspiration grow

Aloha though is all that sounds
like the street catching ears
across the pond outside this
history startled, repeating on

It's over and that's the way
black coffee crows addiction's

suns and moons and starry nights,
just burnt black coals of ocean

Holden

What is it to you, anyway,
pushing the self-destruct button,
just the way it always was?
And now the full-circle reality:

That carousel that never spun –
you did this to yourself,
we did this to you,
because we could never be Jane,
just a huge mass of happy crying Sally's
making all your mistakes again
in your holy atheist name

But none of this matters:
you threw us over the crazy cliff
in love, not with you
but in the selfish pleasure
reading's been since meeting you
in the amber waves of gray December
New York City rye

And that's why I
still love you,
smashing windows
'till these goddam hands
just break

Jersey Sequence

1: Who Goes There?

Who goes there?
The back door unclosed

Mary on the top step,
a window's wind touches

her enough to shiver
But it's everything, right?

2: Clueless Young Lovers

It's all a dream, really – the lonely
curtains let wind fill rooms of emptiness,

something like alive standing in a doorway,
ghost positioning to scream, but silent

while a car goes by outside
driven by clueless young lovers

3: Sandy

Until night, holding out for some sake
that wheels spin sweetly towards alone...

Now drift, current, digest the bitten boards

and wonder if Madam Marie knew these winds.

But quitting is the question, the moon, the pier
crumbled into the ocean and I finally logged off

4: The Point

Dark stars perplex the man
under the universe at night

when sleep won't come inside,
November's sting's the kiss, so

Spin Eliot in no ecstatic circles;
Allen and I have a train to catch

Bottles and Sense

Slow trains miles off
speak like ghosts at four a.m.
and here I am
this is me under a blanket
naked enough
to take the stress away

And then what
but tired repetition
and penitent talks
to mirrors and God
while dogs, outside,
exhale the exhaust
of old pickups
driving away
into sunrise

Traffic flows
almost organic with coffee:
whose anger could rise
against winter sun;
which of these faces,
with eyes and beards,
makeup and travel mugs,
could let impatience win?

ATM screams dollars and cents
for Christmas miracles
and where Santa dazzles
above poor economies,
bulls and bears
fight out native stories

in the stars

An exhausted Stratocaster,
once dormant, awakes and
plays a sold out
audience of one,
objectivist love songs
never scored
sing, finally,
then quiet again,
something else to do

But when the weather breaks,
all these faces find
are self-inflicted symbols
for the drive
and it's up to mirrors
to chew completely the
experience shot back
like Yagermeister
in the night

And it turns out
redemption is
not on some beach's
clear sunrise,
just a whiff of air
while dumping bottles
in the cracked green bin
that smells clean enough
and like potential

All these old folks
jogging, waking, biking,
addition hungry late

but what, then,
of all these babies
in strollers of running
mothers off to work
with bedtime stories
playing like a song
stuck in their heads?

Nine turns to ten:
your bones came up
in the flood last night,
everybody lost and found
but rain keeps
pouring; all I've got
is a ring,
a circle that confuses
fanged monkeys clinging

No more choices
and running's the plan
while strange numbers
from Omaha and Delaware
keep phones ringing
with the costs of youth
and desperate choices
that beg for a hero
yet to take the stage

When the air thickens
and sunrise winds
feel like long past summers,
hope becomes concrete,
the timeless om,
a word, a thing,
so in walking there's

prayer and purpose
beyond dependant breaths

The girl that sits
by the pond,
her body silent, screaming
throaty blues, too old
and too young,
too much and not enough
of this, of that,
just skips a pebble
so the sunning turtle
ducks his head

A long short road
back to the darkest hour,
coffee and the greatest
loneliness of moments,
all the latent good and bad
of what light
the sun may shed,
the steps taking bottles
to the bin

Silence, now,
the post-coital day,
these debts deferred
now singing America
and taken roads await
the dread of rewarding action,
the punishment for the crime,
the sense that comes
from looking into mirrors
and moving on

Speaking

This is it, the first one back
after the beleaguered moment
seemed to have passed

So I shed my cloak,
like the old book says,
still with both hands

I saw the way the dog
spoke wordless to the boy
and thought it mattered

But this matters, too:
if no one were to speak,
there'd be no effort to hear

Hooked

A relapse on TV
and the lonely
knowledge that
the ghost secrets
don't nail palms
and sword sides;
no, they scrape
and prick and let
blood drip and
right when it
really hurts they
bandage sweetly
like Mother's Day
just to start scratching
again at something
that thinks it's alive

The Obvious

What else is there
in between
but silence,

the quiet of years
smiling beyond
the obvious?

This is human;
nothing in nature
would think to ground

electricity, the energy
that smiles silence
over still lips

while minds swirl electron
anxiety oceans
of moments lost.

To ask why is to hurt;
so the silent moments
hold, burst, with grace

Glimpse

Who the stars enlighten
and who the moon sways
into clear midnight water
aren't for me to decide

but when you turned
a second ago to tip
your drink I saw light
wash your face so brightly

that when you pulled off
your lips and dark returned,
I forgot forever who glimpsed
the universe all alone

Tonight, Tonight

Time is never time at all – Smashing Pumpkins

What's it going to be tonight –
beer and Frank O'Hara and the low
drones of exhaustion?

it's in this age,
it feels like rising early
with no place to go

somewhere else
work and family exist
just like pretty holiday cards

but I'm more concerned
with wondering if a pond were alive,
could it drown itself?

so absurdity, hot soup in summer,
lets in the moon, barely bright,
over streetlights and backyard security

Too Many Highway Poems

If perspective would come
from tinted bus windows
maybe I'd know you, sorry,
with all these highways pocketed...

Switched torn and frayed into
new jeans, new roads that
all feel the same with time,
no closer, no further, from you...

So "what do you want for dinner"
and "how was work today"
net the answers of distant roads
and I travel on inert, a sin itself...

When happiness is pretense, badly
played and drenched in dinner drinks,
no food is eaten and two weekends go
by faster than highway windows...

Steps

On some forgotten plane
within a stratosphere
never named,
a step is taken
where heel doesn't hit
first, just a gentle
brace for toes
that breaks boards
still, the creak
a child screaming
as the dog is beaten,
the reverberation
that moves water
still in glasses
by the squished cushions
of an empty couch
and an empty chair

The next step is
as silent as the
mind that moved
the foot in the first place
and, after that,
heels hit first, anyway

Butterflies

Butterflies flicker and fade,
the slow crawl to the light flight,
one of nature's simpler sagas
but those fragile flutters fall
fast, flowers without water
and too much burning summer sun

Inside, with only the dull hum
of a fan through a baby monitor,
I couldn't care less about butterflies
or the rippling pond with horny crickets,
those fattened frogs gator bait
though my money's on the feral cats

They're independent and survivors,
they kill without prettiness but it's beautiful,
destructive without hubris, securely capable
like headlights outside a night black window,
so while you crush tears alone upstairs,
I rest my case on the couch

Flying Away

Morning flight orange
blueing to clarity
the sky of right now

window wing seat eyes,
God's view of the south,
looking for your hand

somewhere holding boys,
milk and morning school
routines, lonely day

makeup, faded skirt,
earrings, pretty face
and they just love you...

Up here, pastel haze;
traveling is Easter,
borne cross born again

down to Atlanta,
your face everywhere,
pond poems released

Mirrors like You

Repetitions inside with every window
wide to autumn open up wide
soul that died are you dead weather
letter office closed no writing now

And where are you, beautiful
against my sins? I'll seek to sleep
on this chair feet up free
while baseball flies away with you

When it's time for pancakes
and winter and your eyes blue
over plans for peace here mirrors
like you won't fly far anymore

Writing

The mosquito
on the bathroom wall
must die
but when I miss
I flush and move on
satisfied with compassion
that comes from
slow hands
and a willingness
to share my blood
with all creatures

Perpendicular Lovers

Perpendicular lovers,
one crashing into
the other, lines
that stop and don't
stop at points
without definitions
of formula math
with their reasons
stemming from data
studied and practiced
and tagged with degrees
that are the antithesis
of love, which
is not graphing paper
but thousands of
scribbles splattered each
day onto a once
white page now
intricately complex
with beauty and boredom
which has exceptions
to all rules because
love has none
from yesterday
that can reasonably
hold up to those
rewritten today
and this is fresh
or free but definitely
not parallel and
not even circular,
just explosive intersections,

perpendicular lovers,
lines that stop
and don't stop at points,
a poem that ends
for now, a girl
needs her back rubbed

Knowledge

1.
your breath rises
beneath me, slides
along my chest,
around my neck,
up, up, and away
into the atmosphere,
spun by a brown fan
somewhere in the sky-
blue painted room
with bright windowed
doors and white sheets

2.
i saw a video
of a star dissolving
into a black hole,
its last exhale
the remnant of light
after leaving the bathroom
in the middle of
the night, which
makes me miss
your breath, trying
for harmony between
natural, emotional,
and intellectual

3.
i don't speak
the language of love;
i only know you

in rooms and cars,
beaches and beds,
know you in ways
a toddler's anxiety
is eased at daycare:
they've left me here
but i'm safe and
when they come
for me there will
be hugs and cookies

4.
as sweat cools,
articulating your beauty
is not a concern,
five senses of knowledge
synthesizing into a sixth
that has something
to do with stars and light
and babies and breath,
looking up to thank
a god I understand
no more yet know
as well, things
start to make sense

Greener Grasses

Over there
across a white
picket freedom,
a mending wall,
the New Jersey Turnpike
north of Exit 11,
that's where
the brown grasses
of loneliness grow

Over there
is where paychecks
burn smiles
that must play phoenix
the 1st and 15th
of every month,
but the phoenix
is lonely and
can pull this off

Over there
grasses burned brown,
independence is
claimed by poverty
as a virtue
while here
selling out is
opportunity,
food on the table

Over there
industrious selves

build unique towers
for debts that
hurt no one
while here, green
kids are slaves
to their fathers'
lonely losses

Over there
lonely only lasts
the absent drive
to the next conversation
while here, surrounded
in the green life
of frenetic motion,
isolation feels
like pressing stones

Over there
they sleep through
nights without worry
for how others
are sleeping or will wake,
while in three a.m.
jitters here wakes
the exhausted acceptance
loneliness bears

Third Person

"I should probably stick
to brown bottles, you know?"

"It's all the same, Sam,
all the same."

A sigh
stems from the history of man,
what work, what age,
brings a bar before sunset:

"These green ones – they let
light in. Ruins it, you know?"

"That's what I heard, Sam,
but who are we to know?"

"I don't know. It makes sense."

"It all does, Sam."

And then
the slow draw is a gun
raised to the lips, it's sweet
fear metallic no bottle
and then falls man
exhausted and just a day
from old

The Last Poet

And it's like that,
a heart breaks but not really,
so connotation's out the window
and he can't go too far

You know what's here,
you know what's gone

The languages are bleeding,
his brothers, his species,
they tell me this in soft pink
tongues soaked in saliva
that turn the phrase,
the brain did it all,
it spoke and we silenced

Poisons for Saturdays,
boys and girls there's nothing left
to shoot

         ***

On Saturdays,
fathers sit in beach chairs
comfortable in sandy wet salt
for castles and solar powered
surf smiles,
watching the kids
and watching the girls
just out of college,
their fresh jobs and gym memberships
don't equal the …

what? Stagnancy? Security?

It doesn't matter,
too many one more beer nights
and the belly's not a six pack,
the tide rises and falls
and the kids play
and the girls tan
and the fathers smile
Saturdays away in water sips
and apples, sweet to cores untouched

This ocean protects, yes, like a mother
for now in sandy salt scrubs,
clean confessional something,
that their circuits just don't understand

He's heard of the death of art
and submission
and he's heard of countryless peace

Considering such electronic elocution,
an ever drunker scribble
sketches ever ancient markings
across the page

                    ***

Subterranean homesick blues
does not compute...Bob Dylan,
Bringing it All Back...nineteen sixty...
music plays, mistakes aren't made
beautiful

Pink robots, we've known it all along,

life, of sorts, imitating art
and now the creation rules
to create a new art,
the new species,
the new biology,
cybernetic meadows

He thinks of these things
and the protective non-love
nestled in a fleshy thigh,
reproductive dreams
and, funny,
life goes on in rhythms

All the great mistakes
we've made them not to make

A bottle of beer, a bottle of wine,
these android pills,
they let us smile, smile, smile...

                    ***

Generations of men
throwing baseballs like language
back and forth, action understood,
negotiations, leather,
the flesh of kinesthetic compromise,
throwing strikes to backstops,
the boy swings, misses,
swings again, misses,
thrown again (he's been waiting)
inside and now conclusive contact,
the satisfaction of the father
(his own would be so proud)

but none of that is voiced
and leather against leather
makes sense

The smells of light breezed spring,
nostalgic, yes,
but also every urge to continue,
to do this again,
to make the next batch better

Generations know generations,
fathers know their shouldered fathers
and watch the cycles spin

Saturdays and Sundays don't exist
because they don't have to
but balls are still tossed
between generations
while updates occur and the sharks are tagged,
traced and left to our devices,
no more harm, it's said,
but the spirit isn't dead, an idea
that's been whispered, too,
and he scribbles down
"I'm no more afraid for me than you"
and what is to do?
Serve the servants, scream the words?

A father takes his teenage years
into working world American lungs,
strums electric emotions
while the boy watches,
not yet quite sure of what's there
behind the noise that hurts
a little but also feels somewhat

alive

Watching, waiting,
generations never speak with words
and the poet stands impressed in envy,
searching for just the right silences
to let the people know,
to let the people go

      ***

Later,
the poet is not of science,
remembering Roethke, even Heaney,
and this does not compute,
synergy and definable compatibility,
dating personals in forgotten papers,
not so bad, not so bad
they say

Destruction never really felt
like anything at all,
no movement to memorialize,
too human, whatever that will mean

Here he is,
a man in dry grass
by a pond that tries to nourish
only it doesn't try,
it just nourishes
and he burns some Walt Whitman
to make a point for the sun,
wiping nervous sweat away,
feeling safe without fingers
touching buttons

but it's the same and ink is sparse,
he wonders if they can
compose without mechanics

And the sting of resentment
makes him see they've got a sort of point

      ***

Headaches tick, tick, tick,
waiting for some virus
that won't stem from exhaustion,
at least not that he has known

Humility and sense of purpose
are battling it out
on the green fields of
self-perception,
but there'll be no more buttons

      ***

This time,
the shameless rise from
the couch, morning
walked, breathing in a day
in absolute correctness

But he's arguing
"it's all wrong"
and no one cares
and he's being watched

So soon the hatred will come
but he can't not care,

can't let that happen
now

Identity confirmed

      ***

Quarantine,
the threat confirmed,
the dream deferred,
never such a thing
as murder

Delete

Isolation identity,
so many times before,
the history of the soul,
the language of the wind,
this has all been recorded,
files stored in backup

What is it to know?
So much information,
action interface,
"annihilation," he thinks,
the drugs are in the wires,
the last proscription

Utter something beautiful,
aesthetics make no sense
no more

      ***

Later that day,
the new frontier,
it's always been here,
songs about paranoid androids,
good art but just a warning
and, there, lies work

A day's work done
but no songs like Whitman,
just more work for home,
sweating, forgetting others,
love saved on file for later use

Secretly at night
the last of the living
go out and fight
each other

Sleep comes to work,
escape the cycle,
birth and death
to create, must destroy,
life comes, prices ring
no dollars matter now,
just time that's faded
away beyond the burst,
circuits and acoustics
that fingers knew

He motions to others
who are identified
and they walk away,
it's all so clear
and meaninglessly simple

This for that,
since the dawn
of civilization,
are these Western Territories
of avoidance
or the greatest freedom
yet?

Brautigan had it right
through imagination but he
knew nonetheless and now
the poet sits in a grassy
open space between
tennis courts and playground,
all watched over,
they measure harm
without abstractions
like love

                ***

But he's allowed
to be and they seem
to think
he might be somehow
needed
as this does not
compute

Sand gets in the circuits
and salty waves will short
the drivers' currents

He joins the dads,
the kids,

the girls

***

Approaching midnight,
only the thinnest sliver moon,
these, the days
to document

His breathing years,
what a man,
gender roles like thunder,
these faces, petals

***

Maintenance needed,
light flashing
with electric power,
backup battery
driving

Help me you know who know how
but that's
in your
control

Self-sufficiency,
old idealists
onto the truth
as much as
humanly
possible

He walks to the pond

ignoring flashing lights

When

Every day goes by,
nothing weighted in beaches
that eat heat lightening and years...

The time for music
of our own won't be now, but
somewhere over this full moon...

Clothes

Clarifying points
is weaponry useful
for communicative
annihilation of self-delusion

and what brings tears
or hurricanes spins out
of the bedroom for
bookless couches

and drinkless rage
that breaks before predicted
landfall uses language
just to dance for grace

and dry eyes stare
into others while hands
hold and bodies touch
bare thighs warming

and temperature drops severe
bring sleep, the unconscious
bodies move into motion
and we wake tearing clothes

and necks are wet while
thoughtless passion pushes
towards sweat and release
and the smiles we need

and this is all that language
couldn't say as we laugh

because the baby woke
three rooms away

So Much Falling Rain

Slow rolling on a rainy Tuesday,
Parcheesi army chaos
while the drizzle down of drops
coats windowed doors
with dreary pretty

One year olds love choke hazards
so we put dice in shakers,
rooks the kings of repetitions
over and over again in perfect
monotonous motions

And this is parenting and
what it means to be a child
and what it means to grow
somehow bright and wild
under so much falling rain

Cave Men

Out here in the world,
cycles spin man-made
regularities, somehow
mirroring nature in attempting
to overcome her

We find caves to cuddle in
and make journeys to others
cowering in the comforts
of walls and temperature,
our bodies pressing something

To return to our cave with
our number marking, keys inserted
and the controlled stillness
of all that is protective, alone,
washes like the sun's rising light

And we, out here in the world,
try to tell the difference
between as good as it gets
and home, a self-constructed
concept that means all of love

Monkeys and Wind

The wind blows
and a shuffling man
finally turns about
face to stare cold
with a storm's eye –
his own central warmth –
all he's (never) known

Crows circle the blues,
black against gray wash,
the absence of clarity
holds its own presence
and the crows are leaves
on the ground circling
in unnamed breezes

The wind blows
and a man spins
again, monkeys and wind
weighing and pushing
along until he turns,
opens wide and breathes
and calls his name

Scrambled Seasons

It's morning so won't you be my Valentine?
There're crushed velvet petals with water and your
        visage

From drizzles to pouring, letting up, a moment passes
        muddy toes,
yours painted light Easter purple to traverse eternal
        Sundays

There's nothing I could be sorry for anymore; not now
with the rain so warm in our hurricane season love

As New Years turn, we choose to kiss without mistletoe
        or eyes;
in the sunlight, the grass glows greener than light across
        the bay

Surrender

The thunderstorm is low
and the rain steady,
it's a good evening for
reading quietly on a couch
gazing up at sporadic
lightning like kids old
enough to play on their own

Earlier we lay for two hours
laughing lightly with gentle touches,
somewhat sleepily planning an afternoon
of errands that don't make much
difference but for the time spent together

But even in the lulling listless
summer storm, all I can see
is you, simultaneously beautiful
in eyes and lips and sensual
in legs and fingers, stretched
across a white bed looking out
at the storm-enlightened pond

We are waiting for love
that's been dormant, dusted
over in anxiety's twisting winds
and debt's pressing stones,
lost in routines that make
good parents, good workers,
good home-owners, estranged friends

So whether it's your eyes or legs
that wrap me in slow thunder

and bright, brilliant strikes,
I surrender, nothing left to lose

Opposing Forces

All seasons speak
this morning,
forty-eight degrees
and overcast,
as much as seventy-two
and humid,
cool and warm pockets,
walking the dog
is moving
through a weekend bar,
so many breaths
making the moment
exactly what it is

Light is coming slow,
gray and still
as inspiration,
the soft kiss
of the right girl
just another step
from sin to salvation
and other ideals
brought by dawn,
the temptress, the tease,
that I'll believe
until work is put off
and five o'clock
is twisted off,
so tomorrow's trip
to the recycling bin
promises something new

Thoughts Strangers May Bear

To voice all dissent
into the swirl
and then breathe it back
in om acceptance
is apparently the secret,
the one no teacher speaks
as when they do
they discredit their role
sort of, language less
than sense in such matters
so the poet wanders off
writing for thoughts
strangers may bear

Us Sonnet

A lone sawmill, a driveway's call,
your girlish wrist, the slow light's approach,
morning window prayers and night's couch,
empty bottle witches around sink cauldron,
food-processor goals – grind away these sins –
love's the coffee that's left, still warm
enough to know twenty-seven degree sunshine,
wedding months and red holidays are a-okay,
the briefcase borne, worker bees poles apart
from heavy eyes, the head rests on the fist,
uncalloused dry like the memory of an ocean,
sandy enough, it was you and me on a towel...
moving on, this quiet street is empty day,
antithesis and angels' silky songs

This Far From Home

Three miles, a long stride
and strength is known,
not simply something
functionally exacted

A long three miles along a long
lonely highway straightening out
the horizon that fades
away to dusk

And the hollow echo truth
is that distance
doesn't even matter
this far from home

Benediction

I hope you find a handsome young man – The Gaslight
Anthem

When Friday night hands
clumsily gripped pens, tired,
the thought of your eyes
guiltlessly swallows pills

because it's late and here
the universe holds itself as is,
so indulgence, subjugated distance,
drinks on into the hours...

what could be more concrete
than the ambiguous fuzz
of strong pills, one for each
breath that dries mouths for you,

as this is the sad you don't see,
gentle images so simple, sushi raw,
but what I really want is sweetness
to take you away from all this...

I wish you a handsome young man,
I wish you to see through good eyes
a love that's worthy of all you are...
you, for you, right now so far...

A Small Breeze

"Everybody's crazy..."

"Listen to you..."

"No. I know these people –
these wives and these husbands."

"Different strokes – that's the theme?"

"But I don't think it should be –
there are always losers who smile nice
and wrong-rubbing winners with power."

a small breeze
is the bored child's sigh
when they don't know anything
somehow sensing it all

"And that's how people are:
smiles and sadness, stones."

"I don't know about that –
everyone knows everything;
that sounds like a good fit."

"But it's not – there are not fits
to fit into."

a small breeze

across a forgotten pond
only moments, anyway

Procrastination

Under the task at hand,
the greatest smiles are born
in ducking out for a snack
that turns into an errand
with a pretty girl and maybe
lunch and then some coffee
because, really, you only
live once, so why not
go back to a bed with white
pillows, white comforters,
and white sheets in a light blue
room with white blinds and
get freaky and then
nice and release for each other
so that in late afternoon the
beer on the porch leads
to another and then whipping up
a light salad to have with something
on the grill and, yes, another
beer, so cold to quench the
post-love cotton mouth and
there was something back there
about a task at hand that
will manifest into a sense of
error that's not what happened
which was E.E. Cummings beautiful
but now my head goes down
which seems like winning,
which seems like sleep

Embers

The stars, they crush me
and these milky streams are
born visible in absent someday
when we all turn off the lights

That's another story, fire,
Prometheus and prayers to thine
own self, the fools and flagrant
referendums bleed to sleep, goodnight

Starlight, bright drunk energy,
poems for the wordless feel of fall
that fingers feebly between the thighs
of every yesterday's sad sung good day

Is it true you and the other?
Windows roll up morning chilly drives
to houses homes and mattress bliss
alone while justice does its best to die

The strange stripped frequencies
left of the dial underground worldwide
whoa, the fire, night and fall
strumming until embers dull to dust

Driving

When the house holds people,
genes and DNA might come up
but, usually, it's just a question
of doors – something to do with cold winds

Seven or so evils down the road,
some winding, single lane through mountains,
that looks like a favorite song played to distaste,
a driver stares at pictures, considering good

That house, miles back by the ocean,
with people, DNA, doors, and questions,
ignites phoenix fires, again and again,
to drive wildly back to in suicidal love

No Man's Land

Like it was a street sign
I could walk past at
5:30 a.m., the dog
no idea this was
the darkest hour

Graffiti by a highway,
the overpass sheltering
so many somebodies
to nobody anymore
and I should care

The response of a waiter
at a diner in the distance
from my booth knowing
he's so mad because
he still cares

Or the mirror of prayer
desperately confessing
what hasn't stopped happening,
hoping for redemption or
to get out of here

Spring Wedding
for Leslie

Stocks and bonds, wars and baseball,
taxes and oil changes and overgrown lawns
are on hold for a wedding in a park

and weddings are happy and should be
like when this and that happened, tugged
and pulled, they found time to whisper,

to kiss, and to smile at their own joke
which made the low-country spring air
even prettier because no one

can explain that, but, when we witness
it, it makes sense and all of our own
details fall into a sort of order

that we wouldn't have otherwise seen
if his black and her white weren't dancing
to "Into the Mystic," the low, muddy Ashley

off behind ancient oaks and local beers,
like the pure fun of girls in nice dresses
jumping into pools they aren't supposed to

just because this is young and alive and now.
The baby will come and life will grow as it does,
so hard, so brutally real, so beautiful

Untitled Thoughts

What one mind says, the spark of action,
is relative to setting and time and circumstance

Of course, I know this so clearly walking alone
before sunrise, sweating for no one and universally
                naked

But this fades away and new identities play Friday
afternoons that call for some entitled indulgence

A stop at the green grocery store breaks budget for beer
and the morning runs fall useless to cream sauce and
                bread

The silence of morning fades to the reckless rambling
of light, cycles repeat and I question the power of reason

Sunburn

No more moon
over white painted faces,
picket fence protests
for just a little light

******** sleep ********

And then sleep
to alarms or just
before the beep,
that nervous awareness

What of actions
and who falls hurt
without the attacker's intent,
traces of escape everywhere?

Attaining ideal
is as easy as whispered
morning prayers,
reassurance against the waking self

No more moon
and the soon rising sun
burns, always burns,
all the paint to true

Old Strings

Heat lightening,
so it seems,
or a storm
building

these old strings
sound so fresh
tonight, the
wind sings

with cicadas
that make
"You Are the Everything"
like prayer

now a storm
approaches pretty
while frogs fuck
on my lawn

what becomes
of power outages
if sleeping sound
all the while?

Drinking Song

Somewhere deep into a bottle
of Italian red (deep)
there's this girl siren calling
but all she does is retreat
the closer I get
(I wanted to use the verb
swim, not *get*, but
I can't explain why)
and this is loaves
of oil and garlic gone
so cramps, of course,
occur when journeys
of the sort are undertaken
and that's where dreams
start from couch cushions
and all the swimming sweats
out of water sheets because
we all know Freudian stress
symbols and who's not overwhelmed
these days it's fucking crazy man
but wait! There she is again
kinda cute but dangerous
and there she goes so,
you know, I gotta go

Wedding Poem

With these things
knowing is
intuitive,
the young legs
of pretty
rich girls bare
for drinking
and dancing
while families
unite smiles

So as shoes
are kicked off,
skirts hiked up,
breasts fall out
while men lose
ties, buttons,
and their minds
all for rules
weddings write
about love

But hey, who's
complaining,
warm rain for
morning breath
and hazy
memories –
nothing did
happen with
that cute girl
anyway

Caterers
aren't supposed
to smile like
that, fingers
urging steps
downstairs to
empty rooms;
turned away
so morning
smiles sweet

Associated Press

Beating the baby moose
had to be done.

What else to do on bicycles,
fifteen?

Because news must be reported
to question ourselves.

"Why are the youth so mean?"
we ask ourselves.

The boys were beaten, too,
or were they not beaten enough?

All the lonely forest heard
was a baby crying for its mother.

And we all know that sound;
authorities put the baby down

If Lao Tzu was my Librarian

Somewhere between wisdom and knowledge,
sense and cognition, intuition and language,
there is the way

and I sometimes wish (when there's
time between checking all sorts of
cool stuff on a myriad of apps)

that Lao Tzu was my librarian,
so maybe I could sit down to tea
and just listen

maybe leaf through what would become
the Tao Te Ching as he hobbled off
unlonely into the woods

but libraries aren't the place to be today
and ancient masters of the eternal way
are burned at social stakes

that's if they exist at all, with so
much knowledge so accessible, it's
got to be hard to be a wise man

Off Somewhere Away

Stacks of papers and all this talk of the end:
it's late May and letters equal numbers,
or the other way around and then assessing is done

So, left to burn (in open sun) is purpose, but
not until the new year (really?) in autumn
and these distractions are identity more than mirrors

Love has fallen into bad geometry, angles
and variables in triangles whose highways
go off somewhere away

A Song

When dark drops, wine spills
on new carpets, dinner dries
though her eyes don't, they
redden in moist now, trying
like little boys who want to hit
but don't, games passing on
won by others all asleep as
awful couples engage awkwardly
like vows all fathers dance for,
mom drunk on the stairway,
heaven here a song for
someone else's key and that's
what turns to icebox bottles
tipped to night's mosquitoes, the noise
of cicadas a silence, just to drown out
those eyes, her disenchanted,
cacophonous eyes...

The Endpoint of Circles

To understand is
to know her face
cracking walnuts
without looking at them,
looking lazy out
some window
I can't even see

A sip of wine,
that tastes okay
but it fits
the budget she's
fine with keeping,
is still confusion:
guilty, failing man

Everyday running to
the endpoint of circles
and nothing but
spring winds that know
winter doesn't die
so, while he's sleeping,
sound the debt of smiles

After the Rain

After the rain,
humidity
and stillness
are only broken
by mosquitoes,
silently desperate
ripples role away

The wet green
contrasts black
clouds still watching
like they've been
for so long,
mud between toes
is infinite history

Interstate mentor,
80 mph over a bridge,
metal girders,
stone and pavement,
no ripples can be seen,
so advanced

Apples

Four apples
not five
(Thursday's pizza day)
remind me
of what I'll
be too busy for
by Friday
and what passes
is gone
and on we walk
alone

Two Pages

When it seems all stories are told,
I read two pages, summer youth
and beads of sweat and why...

She shouldn't have surprised me
but, reminded of youth's rules,
the legs of silence crept away

The shade under evening heat
won't let sweat drip memory;
slowly I surrendered disbelief

Love, Redemption

Love
Redemption

The soul that's morning mist
whose gentle caress
of the glass pond
is as fragile as temptation

Love
Redemption

Time renders picture albums:
old philosophies burn
and only time will tell
if all ash is meaningless

Love
Redemption

Prayers of the tragically hip
answered in only tragedy;
one sun sets, rises,
the essence of humanity

Love
Redemption

Setting

Sometimes,
when the ostrich
pulls out
and shakes Earth's sands,
like a surfer
coming up
on the ocean side
of a wave,
he gets a fuzzy view
of the surrounding
setting and blinks

The bullet hits
like shark teeth
and blood cakes
quick, sand
so unlike
the slow dissolve
in salt water

Another Road Song

The same old road songs,
like a clean ocean's surf,
for wounds that keep opening,
here we go again, I-95

This far south, Florida
fades away from continental worries
and dreams are pretty nothings,
"Cleanse Song," riding waves

Oh, it's you, mirrored maniac
coming back to kill us,
the pleats have broken, you're not sure
what to break and what to mend

My Knees, Your Arms

It's not so much, well,
really my knees ache
but they walk for you

But sometimes, day's end,
I can't read and baseball
cradles me up in treetops

And just like the song
I fall, weighted in avoidance,
then crawl into your arms

Four Directions

What's to say, really,
attempting to guard
four directions at once
leads to thin defense
and then all they see
are holes because the whole
has been portioned into
factions that now argue
ugly into mirrors
where what's seen
are gross distractions,
a blackened storm's eye
blurring with cataracts and
the discrepancies between
what's said and what's done

The pond was Buddha still
until the rain ran it's fingers
along the curves of its lover
only to say wake up, silly,
I feel ignored and you must drink
of me or you'll dry up, too,
and none of these surrounding flowers
will know you calm and full
but just watch you angry, desperate,
fading away, strangling them with distance

So the answers are easy
(they always are):
build damns and
abandon outposts,
conserve water

to nourish that
which needs it
most

Do this and those outposts
won't haunt like Gettysburg ghosts,
where continued effort just bleeds
and no one likes excuses,
especially when you're lonely

Breathing

Every little step towards death –
little stumbles over chair legs
that bump tables and spill
a few sips of cheap morning coffee –
is a breath worth breathing,
a wet spring gently tapping
February's shoulder,
"Hey buddy, it's my turn"
and inhaling that heat –
a sensual tingle suggesting
we head upstairs –
is as good as suntanned skin,
sand exfoliation smooth,
showered under fresh sheets
and a ceiling fan spinning cool,
a friend, a lover, a reason
to breathe moments in season

Doing

Finishing feels like reluctance,
passing off work, sweaty time
stopped, for a result recordable

What's left, in this decided end,
but realization and self-reflection,
mourning the death of sweet process

In early summer's humid breath,
just like autumn behind the door,
I want to sweat, to move, to produce

Something tangible besides mirrors
so the only thought is in the doing;
the doing done, the tide of self comes in

Empty Hats

The rabbits aren't coming;
that's the awful realism,
a dim man's enlightenment,
while staring into empty hats

So the scene opens, empty street
and, out of nowhere, it's outside overcast
and the man watches his lonely walk away,
top hat bluster blown to backwards ball cap

This all takes place on a public path
paved through grass and streetlights
and stringy trees planted after bulldozers
left and there his I goes after all away

What else now that wooden bats crack
after such seasoned use and now batting
the stands have filled with October chills,
strikes and balls and walking away for someone else

Inside Outside

A wooden chair
on a concrete porch,
shrubs, grass, pavement,
grass, pond, tree line

But what I missed
was the glass door,
carpet, coffee table,
feet, legs, me

This is what is
was, now, soon
always separated by
unopened transparent doors

Angels

"We're all supposed to be angels" she says
with a soft sigh, aware of angels' weight
I lean back and sigh, wishing for windows
or a nice patch of sand (really, a beer)
but I have this job, and I no longer
can scream wild anthems, I've decided this
because money is food and I'm no good
man, just an aging child set'ling into
a comfortable routine, day in, day
out and who am I to dig into her
today, my yesterday, all the sweet same
"We are, too" I manage to utter
glancing down, then back to R.E.M. eyes
"Things keep happening, we go on" I say
unsure of the depth I wasted, wanting
to at least respect her with a profound
word or two that would stand for great wisdom
"I'm O.K." she says "I am one – it's them
that I can't stand" with a shrug to somewhere
just over her shoulder. "Well, gotta go."
"K. Have a good one" I say to the wall,
of course she will, an angel after all

Born to Run

We gotta get out while we're young – Bruce Springsteen

How does blood boil?
I need to know only because
long desperate nights have made choices
the man I longed to be
wouldn't ever think to choose
and now, mourning almost light,
I'm left with the responsibility
for building towers
(or leveling them – I'll get back to you),
to dust return, I know, I've heard
there are places down these highways
jammed with broken heroes
and all the fear
these hands have ever created

There is blood still that I could let
for you, so here's my soul
to walk with in the sun,
here I am, one more last chance,
make me know that love is real
and the rest of this will go away
or so I say while running
with you through the dreams
of another day

Falling Asleep

Is it so easy, forgetful old (young)
man asks himself, after the day
of observing faces cruelly devour
each other, alligator patience
for the unfailing snap,
to move to the pack's peak?

Are you aware?

Yes, but the soft approach is seductive
and the mind divides, the world
above and the world below the ice
incommunicado

Tomorrow I'll be better, tomorrow
things will get done
(tomorrow, we're all superheroes)

But the bed leaps up,
pulls dreams too quickly
leaving too many of Frost's apples
on the bough, covers are flying,
ice cream's churning and...

Anxiety Attack

It sure felt free
vomiting into two a.m.,
birds neurotically
singing something Lysol
and cold feet couldn't
bring to the mirror

And after all that,
fever dreams and nausea,
colleagues and debts drifting
away on islands,
split Pangaea, all so fast,
the work day looms
four, five, six a.m., and what
the body says goes

The couch, the windows,
and every neighbor mowing;
I couldn't work
so the lasting knowledge
that this land
was not made for me
lulls me under fans
and something sick

Thoughts Listening to Thievery Corporation

What busy means is escaping me but not quickly, not as quickly as the '82 Toyota minivan with no muffler disappearing in the dust of faces, faces all so brown and pretty with purpose, not as dead as December New Jersey with all those mini-mall smiles, this is something more than the absence of suburban faces cramming together under credit-card days of stops for boutique lunches because this is where there isn't any nothing and I'd like to know something about that but it may have been so quickly fastened to the so quickly fleeing '82 Toyota minivan – it was silver – and I can't make out the license plates just the white winded curtains, cloth, shades stained with sandy brown (that's all there is) and stuck in trances people look look look me into corners uncomfortable silences watching answers speed themselves away…

Dawn or dusk must be down that alley around fading, fleeing time and it occurs to me to check for sewage, drainage, anything but there is only absence which doesn't work with all the clutter, why I once spoke of what busy means and lost it just as quickly as everything else that's gone before, the woman in black her hair was Hell she stared at me as a mother and knew all mother sides of my stories I couldn't then spit out, my tongue dried dusty silent…There's the van! She stared me still and down another driving distance where what this all means goes away while I wanted everything I wanted to know what busy means but it quickly cut the scene is black and sound is just an '82 Toyota minivan without a muffler going, going gone…

Chasing Down What's Choking

A spectacle – it always is –
and tanks are filled with
belly dollars the drinks would,
of course, have to sacrifice
since, you know, it's for
the cause, the entitlement
we have to smile, smile, smile
breathing not for seconds
without the beeping brilliance
that needs charging some
times, too, and so to sleep
but dreams are rancid, they
taste like guilt and fear,
which is to say like tin
foil paraphernalia and a
woman late at night, but
I believe in something
stronger, something yelled
from Springsteen's lungs
or the wind off Vlad Guerrero's
bat and all this lets me
know is that it's weakness
that's the burden and
redemption's just another choice
I'll say until the world
lights up its own ideas,
it's a spectacle – it always is –
chasing down what's choking
with eyes that swagger like an ass
on some girl that is the
unfinished thought before sleep

Yawn

The lawn lets Sunday go
as wine glasses break
on the same pavement
boys' bare feet tread

1996 was the year
and how time moves
or doesn't mirrors still
quiet yells and yawns

Bulldozer

What part of the day brings a thirty-three
year old man to ask, like a late-night kid,
what's this all really mean, anyway?

There's a blur that's more intuitive
than concrete and this ebb and flow is social,
part of our construction, part of our being.

There's a blur in the man working
to incompleteness that is covered off
the clock and his friends have stopped

bothering to call, like the child who's
stopped bothering to look up to the man
he calls father who's stopped hearing son.

When the rocks are manmade steel,
even saxifrage can't break through,
the snake and grass bulldozed long ago

Night Singing

I'm not sure all these people understand – R.E.M.

There isn't a lot to remember,
her voice now is a ghost
of memory – good, bad,
I guess it all depends

A year or so of Saturdays
washing away work weeks,
trips to the store
for drinks and how to make them

The kids would drift to sleep
and out back, me first
strumming away to the first beer
while the backyard filled with smiles

But it's her that I remember
(it's how we passed the time),
the moon arcing over morning
eyes alight with fire's moves

What could be more beautiful
than a memory glorified,
strained pangs for Jane Gallagher
eased in a song?

Conversations for Creation

"These happinesses kill" she said
and it wasn't just the room,
all those carpets, aged wood,
faded rainbows only shining brown
and she wasn't talking, either,
about cigarettes (she quit last year),
just timing, running red lights

"I can make this magic" she said
and she believed beyond now
that she would and could do
just that – play the cards for smiles,
aces, aces everywhere
but here

"It's these eyes of mine" she said
but she meant the way she acts
when mirrors aren't around and
lonely flashes cat claws at the night

"Sunrise is always saddest, anyway."

Fingers

The road always went somewhere,
dissolving into each town that absorbed,
where one conversation ended...
our fingers were there
and what else can be known?
that touch of infinity, of summer,
no advancement of mind has language
to say where things left to...
those late night sweated goodbyes
shouldn't play into our fingers,
so ice cream melts and white wine warms
but rocking chairs outside sway
like grandmothers' crosses –
what do these knees know, now,
except to carry the meal
of inertia, the conflict of self
in place and in others,
petals on a wet, black bough?
sure, but each one loved by someone
like lightning over the ocean
and that's why when I think of Jersey
an old car comes to mind
and fingers that let roads dissolve
with the purpose of getting somewhere,
when the radio knew the answers
we'd all grow up to hide
while driving late at night windows
breathing in the way your fingers smile

Girl Jazz

To her health
because what else
is there?
The light switch
won't flick itself
off at night, so
antihistamines
and a few beers
are power,
that voice of hers
talking into Miles Davis
rainy drives,
and it's known this
is yesterday
claiming tomorrow
for every sip's
a soft snare's step
into sweetness

The Loneliest Knowledge

Morning comes winter streaked
in wet gray weight that
smells like baseball and hope

Spring is part awareness,
change hinging on responsible,
chance out there on the mound

Winter, still, sunrise,
the illusion of warmth
is the inspiration to live

All ponds contain ocean
and every man, mankind:
this, the loneliest knowledge

Reading Roads

Finished Matt Dillon's audio *On the Road* –
then went looking for Cassidy's history
but found Ginsberg who I'd been
away from, but just as quickly found
Snyder and thought of *Dharma Bums* and
how happy terrifying those lonely woods
must have been, unlike sad lonely *Big Sur*
sea – from these search engine blues
to the book shelf, breezing through lines
in old mirrors to find Li Po,
opened to pages where both poems
were to Tu Fu, and look at that
wild connection! So flipped to Ginsberg,
where this almost started but went
to late eighties pages (May 1-3, 1988) –
or how back on 12/2/87 at 4:30 a.m.
he wrote to Jacob Rabinowitz that
"2000 years after Catullus, / nothing's
changed poets or politics" and in this
I feel comfortable and perfectly unsafe –
and he thinks of "editor's stylistic
competence" for a history of his generation,
friends a studied academic movement
and this brings me back to Neal / Dean
contemplating time like Siddhartha,
Hesse I'll soon be teaching once again…

Heartbeat

A heart can stop
so excuses become
bad TV and someone
else's radio sweltering
at a traffic light
while the only purpose
ever was to go
to the beach

The heart that still beats
after bottles bear dragons
is the one I'll slur songs with
as the sun also rises

Chances

Both of us, I think, think of chances,
hare nap opportunities,
the ecstasy of shared victory
as if the eloped love
of a few eternal hours
in some little beach house
where it's warm but not so hot,
sunset and sunrise the only time,
could hold forever
like a baby grasps its blanket
settling safely into sleep

Chances occupy thought...

There's the quiet mountain cottage
so-far-away-from-people beautiful,
the snowy white reflected sun
ruddying cheeks and toes that
hot fires, the heat of starving bodies,
will bring peace to
like a mother and nursing child
settling safely into sleep

Chances are everywhere,
no lottery long shot,
so, I think, we both think
of moments
when time has no future
and actions fall to the enchantment
irresponsibility provides,
like Quinn the Eskimo
or Mr. Tambourine Man,

luring us into empty depths,
the bliss of LaLa Land...

But thinking of chances,
we don't have to wake up,
which keeps every little thought perfect,
hangovers being such wasted effort,
regret being such a poorly written song,
people's perceptions being such acute reality,
all never part of the chances,
left so picture-perfectly untaken
that, I think, we both think of
getting the chance to take

Sleeping Bad with Jersey

The empty beer, the morning light,
the distance deemed right sleeping bad,
shirtless bodies, covered dreams,
cracking voices break the beams, her eyes
dry, the broken hearted, all the pills will
sleep for sound, sleeping bad New Jersey,
tonight, the boardwalk splinters everything,
your phosphorescent eye liner, kiss the switch-box,
Ferris Wheels in still frames, transit trains
unearthed for the season, ecstasy
and the sun so far from here, horizon
hand over the bedside, a hand held to
last night, the shady shadow hooded,
he was just a boy, the carnival emblazoned
in blue eyes, Ferris Wheels and buzzers,
frayed jeans lean on skee-ball alleys,
cigarettes so soaked with summer, it's all here
or it was, sleeping bad with Jersey,
left her for the morning light, the empty
beer, the distance deemed right sleeping bad,
eye-lids blinking years back from the dead,
the books, the broken hearted,
answers spin in Ferris Wheels, office ties,
the suit that strangles sweat shirts in the sand,
New Jersey sleeping shirtless soundless,
dreamless through the night so terrifying,
boardwalk buzzers, pregnant girls
walk skee-ball alleys, cluster headache heart break,
water's really in the bottle, that pierced tongue's
not so figurative now, sleeping sounds so silent,
all the pills, the shore's been snowed on,
blankets on the floor, laundry basket chaos,

it's all here New Jersey sleeps alone,
whispers what she mumbled once to me,
it's all the same, scraped a knee hopping benches,
splinters in the morning, sad scene sand,
eyes feigning alive, the empty beer, the light
of age-stained morning, distance, horizon
on the ocean, a walk away, fresh air,
the empty beer, sinister caress,
she blinks, it was for me, covers gone
the whole room's gone to hell,
broken radio, window view too clear to see
the light, the boy ran away to taste the day,
she'll be sleeping soundless singing
morning songs of shirtless summers,
the empty beer, who's that by her side? Ferris Wheel,
free ride,Tilt-a-Whirl, night terrors,
Zipper romance bulbs are broken, yellow car needs oil,
tan legs, New Jersey sleeping bad, the empty beer,
the shirtless bodies broken hearted, all alone,
the light of age-stained morning,
I woke alone without her...

The Winds of Seventeen

I thought somewhere
back across twenty-something
to an intersection where
I asked the universe
the way and got turned right

But I don't trust
the winds of seventeen
anymore, too many voices
interfering in the airwaves,
all my own, up here

Three Segments

torn seams and fraying jeans,
dreams, the bricks of Babylon
but it's just the suburbs with
faded blue aluminum siding,
grassy greens and brown streaks
appear as moss on wooden posts
once white, once white

he walks around the edges,
clovers look so pretty lying down,
the wind is autumn,
a dry leaf passes, zombie shuffle,
no more one more time around,
sighs and silence, headache,
breathing, no one wants a frown

morning stretches, the only thing
that matters is the next step
then the next one, they'll
start to see, he'll never have
to speak, tie the laces,
leash the dog, everybody's watching,
nothing's on, the sun will be up soon

To the Mailbox

When will these winged monkeys
quit their incessant circling
of my cold bare autumn feet?

When it's coffee I need,
mornings are distracted absences and
work's a small town express train passing

Red-headed ducks and tourist geese
shake me down for the crumbs
credit cards left outside of ball parks

This is all to be taken in breaths
as the man carries his sins to the mailbox,
each stride longer, lonelier than the last

Stars Go By

So the stars go by and
it seems the illusion is
beautiful so to think
of time O'Hara and Tu Fu
blend in some wild welcoming
beard of Whitman's that
draws eyes like Northern Lights
I've never seen but dreamed
so thank God for film
and the recording of music
and Gutenberg of course
as all I ever thought
to breathe was stained pages
but that's okay as lungs
and heart and brain
work with six senses
to digest what has
made the difference for
all those hours I've had
on a porch by a pond
watching stars go by

When Summer Comes

When summer comes
all these footsteps –
the stomped snow tracks
of trailing Sasquatch –
might disappear in smoothed sands
with the next low tide

When summer comes
all these words –
frozen in the roles of man
sharp as each success –
might warm so sun-burned boys
can raise Excalibur

When summer comes
all these screams –
stems that sink to stresses
irresponsibility sucks dry –
might slow to silent sighs
and save a wintered soul

When summer comes
the same old songs –
salvation in some far off distance
singing sins for reconciliation –
so scratched the years of use
are the only sound

The Language of Kindness

If all you wanted
was the language of kindness
I could have written
songs like parables,
lilies turning seasons
sixties voices couldn't sing

But under what alters
would your blues turn
like seekers of the sun's
life, mother start
that lights God's night
then turns away?

Where Casting is Easy

When night brings dragons
and empty bottles, then
diffusing flames is out
of the question and
all the hope in the world
is the next common stare:
so that's it for Everyman;
the steps were bold but
we've all sharp stones from
beside these couches where
casting is easy, safe, and real

To Speak in Tongues

So much death before rising,
boulders beyond man's strength
not, really, even his weighted will…

But what else is Easter for
if not to know death,
the doors it can open?

These stories are not known
by Catholic children told to know,
memorize, and celebrate miraculous

There's so much living before death
and what boy knows strength
that doesn't have to do with sport?

But that's wrong, there…boys
have fathers, and nothing takes more
endurance than living with their dying

We all want boulders shed
like cloaks while borne crosses burn
in redemptive flames of new breath

But no one else moves the boulder
(that was in the stories, too)
and to speak in tongues…try

November Poem

So we all lined up
and made our choices,
cast our stones,
definite actions, net results

How could I have missed
the differences in doors,
home we call by place
like numbers and maps exist?

Then that stretch of I-95
opened up and I returned,
somewhere along the way
it became possible

Meteors over Russia

It's those stars again
that swirl like meteors over Russia
in the daylight, stamping
"poet" and I just look for mirrors

"No more!" I heard Ginsberg mad
(as he could be) and I had to
say something like a yell
but I growled, no howl or yawp,

like some existential excuse my
learned self scoffed at, but the
old soul that's been the good me
just gets sad reading novels

and so I'll break form, Allen,
but just know it's not for you,
just because of...

Halitosis

Halitosis – it's yours
and the steamy heat
is all over the internet

This is low-country
midnight summer garlic
and March's lion sleeps

Baseball begins, so hope,
but I'm not young (I am),
so scared of self divided

What this man says
and what this man does,
seasons, suns, moon, time

Passing and clicking information
bit by bit, a non-memory of
drugs being so much better then

Breath from screams and dreams
are paranoid terrors, failure
and the man I thought to be

Rocking chair with no man there,
the question of stillness
a lion about to wake

A Stone's Throw

In every light, darkness,
something we've known
since Lao Tzu and back

and yet it is the role
of a human being in light
to draw up another's dark

like drawing up a winter blind
so the snow white bright
does as much as blind a man

now without darkness or friends
whose sad solace burns
"I'm just like everyone"

When it Rains

Oh, there you are
how are we going to get through this one?

And where do you run off to
when it rains?

What of little boys feeding ducks
sunflower seeds, almost falling from muddy banks?

Sunburnt time, the awareness of faults,
and in you came, singing, smiling...

No room left in here for you; but where
do you run off to when it rains?

Question for Geese

Summer hit at around 12:44 today
and by 8:15 things have settled,
staring into the old pond, the only
question on my lips for the two
families of geese, one with teenagers
and the other with fuzzy toddlers:

I've been watching you guys
foraging for food, hissing at
the intrusive humans addicted
to the innocence they've abandoned,
so how do you do it? There are
gators and feral cats everywhere,
and here you are settling down
peacefully, corralling the kids
without stifling them, watching
the still pond take in the hazy
sweetness of summer's setting sun...

The Last Drag

Can you look me straight in my eyes
And tell me love is forgiven? – The Samples

There's a whisper, long silenced,
trying to scream but only sleep
happens; another day fades away...

I watched a bright sun setting
driving straight into beautiful fire,
only that and nothing more...

You know what's wrong now, you
can't deny this but for how long?
and please God one more chance...

www.ingramcontent.com/pod-product-compliance
Lightning Source LLC
Chambersburg PA
CBHW021930040426
42448CB00008B/1000